Early 18th-century English Glass
Frank Davis

The New Metal	3
Variations on Several Themes	9
Drawn Stems and Amen Glasses	28
The Techniques of Engraving	40
The Trade and the Government	49
The End of an Old Fashion	56

COUNTRY LIFE COLLECTORS' GUIDES

Covered jug. The 1720s. Victoria and Albert Museum, London.

Acknowledgements

Photographs were kindly supplied by the following: Ashmolean Museum, Oxford; British Museum, London; Christie Manson and Woods Ltd, London; Corning Museum of Glass, New York; Guildhall Museum, London; London Museum; National Portrait Gallery, London; Pilkington Glass Museum, St Helens; Radio Times Hulton Picture Library, London; Sotheby and Co., London; Victoria and Albert Museum, London.

COUNTRY LIFE COLLECTORS' GUIDES

Series editor Hugh Newbury
Series designer Ian Muggeridge

Published for Country Life Books by
THE HAMLYN PUBLISHING GROUP LIMITED
LONDON · NEW YORK · SYDNEY · TORONTO
Hamlyn House, Feltham, Middlesex, England

EARLY 18TH-CENTURY ENGLISH GLASS
ISBN 0 600 43601 2
© The Hamlyn Publishing Group Limited 1971
Printed by Toppan Printing Co. (H.K.) Limited, Hong Kong

Goblet. Thistle bowl, hollow mushroom and ball-knopped stem. About 1705. Height 6⅝ in.

weight and to attract custom by other means. In this sense one can argue that taxation proved a stimulant, encouraging manufacturers to look about them and find attractive substitutes for the well-tried fashions of the past. But the probability is that these or similar changes would have come about in any case; fashion is an unpredictable jade obeying no set rules apart from the very broad one that what is the last word in one decade can seem very old hat in the next. Whatever the stimulant, the next half-century witnessed the perfecting of some remarkably pretty tricks, notably a great variety of colour twists in the stems of wine glasses, a notable, short-lived blossoming of enamel painting by the Beilby's (brother and sister) of Newcastle, and a great development of cutting both in England and in Ireland. One can still hold to the theory that the best of the English glasses were the majestic baluster-stem goblets of the first half of the 18th century while admitting that, in the second half, the industry, having found its feet, and a far wider market, produced some of the gayest, most graceful table glass ever known.

Two members of the Kit Kat Club. By Kneller. About 1710. The first Duke of Newcastle and the seventh Earl of Lincoln. Slender baluster wine glasses. National Portrait Gallery, London.

evolutionary changes undergone by the baluster form. On the other hand, the light balusters were the specialised product of one, or possibly two provincial factories only, and one in which the style remained practically unchanged for well over half a century; they were important enough, however, to enjoy international reputation.

'There are other distinguishing features between balustroids and light balusters. I include in the former group all knopped glasses made by the two-piece method only [where the stem and bowl are made from a single piece, the one drawn out from the other], whereas light balusters of Newcastle manufacture were mainly fashioned by the three-piece method [the bowl, stem and foot being made separately]. It does not necessarily follow, however, that balustroids were not made in Newcastle glass; the line drawn between the balustroids and light balusters refers to style, not to provenance. The metal itself is also an indication whether a glass should be designated a balustroid or a light baluster; the metal of the light baluster is particularly water-white in colour, clear, and of a brilliancy that is unmistakable once it is recognised. If further assistance is needed in distinguishing between the two styles of glasses, the presence of the folded foot is a helpful guide taken in conjunction with other features, the fold being usual with balustroid glasses but exceptional with the Newcastle light balusters.' The author made a most valuable contribution to the study of his chosen subject, but in my opinion insistence upon rigid differences of this nature can leave the neophyte a trifle puzzled.

What is established is that the baluster gradually lost its imposing character and thinned down to a slender stem, as in the glass which the Duke of Newcastle is holding in the famous painting **Two members of the Kit Kat Club**, in the National Portrait Gallery. The Duke was killed in the hunting field in 1711, the painter Sir Godfrey Kneller died in 1723, and the club itself was in existence between 1688 and 1720. One can therefore date the painting to about 1710.

It remains to give some indication of later developments. The Excise Act had made it essential for glassmakers to cut down

Trade card of John Burroughs whose 'Glasse house with out Ludgate' may have been that referred to in Pepys' diary for 23rd February 1669. Burroughs was Master of the Glass Sellers Company in 1681-1682. The engraving shows a furnace in an elaborate classical frame, with the proprietor facing us and the 'gaffer' seated in his chair with his 'pontil' on the arm and a gathering of molten glass at the end. Late 17th century.

Early type of octagonal decanter-jug. The 1720s. Victoria and Albert Museum, London.

The baluster—the heavy baluster that is—was popular chiefly from about 1700 to 1730, while the so-called Silesian stem, already mentioned as coming in with the house of Hanover, was in use until about the middle of the century. The heavy baluster developed into a much lighter shape, the stem becoming longer and more slender, the type being generally referred to as the pedestal or balustroid. A good deal of what seems to be unnecessary hair-splitting has been caused by making a distinction between the light baluster and the balustroid. However, both descriptions have come to stay, and E.M. Elville (*English Tableglass*) saw yet further differences between them:

'The balustroid was a national style, and portrays the natural

Cruet bottle. An early example of cutting. About 1740. Victoria and Albert Museum, London.

glassware of all kinds was frequently sold by weight, not by the piece. Here are two advertisements from the *Tatler*, the first from the issue of 5th August 1710, the second from that of 26th September of the same year. 'At the flint glasshouse in White Fryars, are to be sold all sorts of **Decanthers**, Drinking Glasses, **Crewits**, etc., or Glasses made to any pattern, of the best flint at 12d. per pound.' 'Drinking Glasses, Decanters, Cruits, etc. There having been of late many advertisements published of flint glass sold at some particular places at 12d. per pound; 12d. per pound is the current price the shopkeepers of London and Westminster do sell at. And all gentlemen and others may at any of the said shops have any sort of flint glasses (and glasses made to any pattern) at 12d. per pound.'

58,59

Goblet. Wide bowl, inverted baluster stem, heart-shaped tear. About 1695. Height $8\tfrac{3}{4}$ in.

The End of an Old Fashion

So much has been written about the design of glasses during the past twenty-five years that the beginner is liable to lose heart when asked to memorise the twenty-eight different shapes of bowl, the twelve forms of foot and the twenty-three types of stem so lovingly listed by the late E. Barrington Haynes in his exhaustive study *Glass through the Ages*. I have to confess that I sympathise. Such meticulous treatment can discourage all but the most dedicated and can, unless he is reasonably strong-minded, turn him into a pedant learning more and more about less and less rather than into a connoisseur sensitive to the subtleties of this marvellous material. However, in order to keep his mind reasonably tidy without cluttering it up with overmuch detail, the following list may serve as a guide to the chief features of English glass during the first forty or forty-five years of the 18th century. The dates, it must be understood, are only approximate, for fashions, whether in glass or hats or furniture, changed but slowly, and what might have been the last word in London in 1710 could well have been considered the height of fine taste in the Midlands or the North ten years later.

We begin then with heavy, majestic glasses in the newly discovered formula in the last years of the 17th century, their value in those days determined by their mass rather than by anything else. The normal stem would be an inverted baluster, but there were numerous ingenious permutations of this or that type of knop. Weight, though not everything, was of importance, for

left Four light table candelabrum. Domed and terraced foot. About 1695. Victoria and Albert Museum, London.

right Goblet. Engraved with diamond-point. About 1705. Height 10⅝ in. Victoria and Albert Museum, London.

below Sir Thomas Saunders Sebright, Bart., Sir John Bland, Bart., and two other gentlemen smoking and drinking. Signed and dated 'B Ferrers pinxit 1720'. Collection of Mr and Mrs Robert Tritton.

nothing, perhaps because the trade was sufficiently well-established to bear the tax, and sufficiently ingenious to sidestep its effects. It is, however, pertinent to note that the period between these two Acts (the years covered in this book) witnessed the finest half-century of the craft in these islands which may, or may not, indicate (according to one's political theories) that glassmaking reaches a higher standard when not singled out for the sinister attentions of the tax man.

custom was for men to be engaged for a term of three to seven years, and to be guaranteed forty weeks work a year. Another sidelight into conditions is revealed in these late 17th-century documents: 'Many hundreds of poor families keep themselves from the Parish by picking up broken glass of all sorts to sell to the Maker'. No doubt there is some exaggeration here as in other propaganda, but there is also a solid basis of fact. Broken glass (cullet) was collected in an organised manner, and it was a scarce though important commodity; it is a necessary ingredient in every pot of metal, as useful as steel scrap in the steel industry. It has already been noted that while pottery fragments are common finds when foundations for a new building are excavated in London, broken glass, even rough bottle glass, is a rarity.

The Excise Act of 1745 imposed another heavy burden upon the industry. Again there was an outcry but this time it achieved

Early 18th-century wine bottles. Greenish glass.

the duty was reduced by one half. By then the French war (the ostensible reason for the duty) had ended with the Peace of Ryswick in 1697, and a year later, by the Act of 4th May 1699, the entire duty was abolished and the industry left undisturbed for forty-six years. Thorpe, delving into the various petitions with which Parliament was bombarded during these four years, reaches the following conclusions.

There were about eight hundred persons employed in the trade, divided among sixty-one or sixty-two glasshouses. Two-thirds of the total output was manufactured in London. Glasses were sold to the public either by weight or by number. And in London there was a body of foreign 'Artist Glassmakers', mainly from Italy and the Netherlands, distinct from the English workmen. The latter complained of low wages 'considering the heat and slavery of their work' as compared with other trades. The

But if the Treasury was disappointed the glass manufacturers were outraged and brought every possible pressure to bear upon the Government. Petitions rained upon Whitehall and anyone remotely connected with the business worked himself up into a fine state of indignation, not wholly without reason, for if a duty was to be levied upon a promising manufacture 20% seemed excessive—and, with the experience of nearly three hundred years behind us, seems so today. As usual the outcries did not err on the side of moderation. Honest men would be thrown out of work, wives and children would starve, small enterprises would inevitably go under and the only people to benefit would be the big men with sufficient capital to work on a large scale. The whole thing, it was suggested, was a put up job on the part of a few individuals with large investments in joint-stock companies deliberately out to destroy liberty and to feather their own nests. Amid all these insinuations and appeals to the emotions a few hard-headed, down-to-earth types produced some figures which Thorpe quotes in his account of this episode. Before the Act came into force the gross value of *all* glass manufactures was estimated at £63,000 per annum, and the net profit to be expected from the duty £11,600. The accounts of the Excise Commission for the period between Michaelmas 1695 and November 1696 revealed the gross produce of the tax as £17,642 1s. 5d., less colliery charges of £7,769 13s. 1d.—that is a net sum of less than £10,000. The original Act was to be effective for a term of five years, but a further Act in 1696 confirmed its predecessor and abolished the time limit, confirming also the fears of the trade.

At the end of 1697 Parliament, badgered by so many petitions, appointed a committee to investigate the industry. The committee took evidence from employers and workers, great and small, and from many districts. For instance William Jackson testified that as a result of the tax he and his partners had been compelled to shut down their glasshouse in King's Lynn, and his evidence was supported by practical men from Stourbridge, Gloucester and the North Country. As a result the committee concluded that the industry had suffered because of the tax and that the Government had derived little or no benefit from the revenue. In August 1698

English glasshouse making bottles. An engraving by Henri Gravelot, the French artist who was working in England between 1733 and 1745.

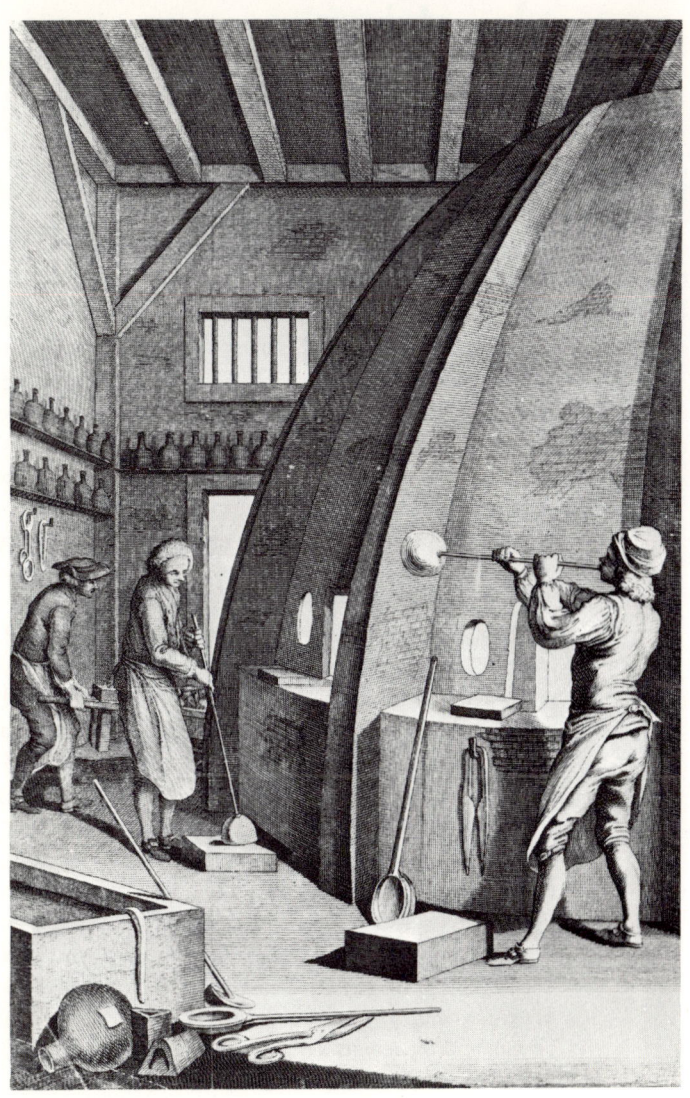

The Trade and the Government

Before going further into the ill-documented story of the glass industry during the first half of the 18th century it would be as well to consider two occasions when the trade indulged in a dispute with the Government. In the first of these, after four years of turmoil, it scored a great success. In the second it failed to make any impression and therefore devised ingenious means to overcome the handicap imposed upon it. By a coincidence the first dispute happened at the beginning of the period covered by the present little volume while the second came at the end and, also by chance, at the time of the 1745 rebellion which, for quite other reasons, seems a convenient date at which to close this account.

It is clear enough that by the mid 1690s glass manufacture was an expanding industry and that the English lead glass or flint glass (the two terms were used indiscriminately) had a considerable future. Inevitably King William's advisers, casting about for additional sources of revenue, took a close look at the glasshouses and decided they were ripe for plucking, together with such older trades as earthenware, stoneware and tobacco pipes. The results were disappointing for both the Treasury and its victims. By the Excise Act of May 1695, to be effective from September of the same year, **green glass bottles** were to pay a tax of a shilling a dozen, and flint glasses and glass plates of all kinds 20%. The Treasury found that the entire proceeds from the glass duty between Michaelmas 1695 and November 1696 were less than £10,000 and so hardly worth the cost of collection.

the Victoria and Albert Museum, one engraved with the story of Perseus and Andromeda, and bearing the crowned initials of the Elector Christian II of Saxony (died 1611) and of the wife he married in 1602, Hedwig, daughter of Frederick II of Denmark. The two other panes, dated 1619 and 1620, are engraved on the wheel, but are unpolished, and the designs not given emphasis by diamond-point highlights as became common practice later in Germany. It is scarcely necessary to add that Lehman worked on the Venetian type of metal (soda glass). Towards the close of the 17th century German experiments, parallel with those of Ravenscroft in England, succeeded in producing a fine, clear crystal glass (containing potash instead of soda, and a large proportion of chalk) which was found to be very well suited to cutting and engraving—yet another good reason, apart from a very natural conservatism, for not adopting the English formula.

Goblet. Wheel-engraved and with the motto of the Walpole family, '*Fari quae Sentio*. Prosperity to Houghton'. Cut glass stem. About 1740. Height $7\frac{5}{8}$ in. Garton Collection, London Museum.

Sweetmeat glass. Wheel-engraved fluted bowl, Silesian stem. About 1730. Height 6½ in. Garton Collection, London Museum.

copper wheel... An abrasive mixture of oil with emery or carborundum powder is smeared upon the edge of the wheel, and the glass brought into contact with it, the slightest touch being sufficient to grind a dull, greyish-white mark upon the glass. The wheels used are interchangeable and of great variety, the larger ones being about 4 inches in diameter, up to a quarter of an inch in thickness, and the smallest not much larger than a pin's head. The edges are bevelled in various ways and are prepared by the craftsman himself; much of his skill depends on their preparation and selection. Unless the engraver is an exceptional craftsman, it is customary to mark out the design upon the glass with a mixture of gum and chalk. The heavier portions of the design are then roughed out, a coarse grain of emery and a wide wheel with a flat edge being used for this purpose. As the design develops, the wheels are changed and a finer grade of emery used to add the detailed work in the design. In the case of a decoration requiring different shading effects, wheels of lead, wood, cork, or rubber are employed to give varying degrees of polish to the engraved surfaces.' It is important to realise that it is the wheel that is fixed and the glass to be engraved is moved in the hand. It is, in short, the lapidary's technique employed not on jade or agate or a dozen other suitable hard stones, but on a more fragile material with exceptional qualities of refraction when a single slip can bring disaster.

Engraving on gems and carving on rock crystal had long been familiar when, for the first time, Caspar Lehman (1570–1622) first used his lapidary's wheel on glass at the court of that remarkable character Rudolf II, avid patron of the arts and politically inept emperor, who shut himself up in his castle at Prague with a notable menagerie of handsome women, brilliant scientists (among the latter the astronomers and mathematicians Tycho Brahe and Kepler), astrologers, wild animals and a sprinkling of disreputable adventurers. One work actually signed by Lehman has survived. This is an armorial beaker decorated with figures and flowers after an engraving of 1597 and, after the engraver's signature, the date 1605. There is another beaker dated 1592 which is believed to be an early work by him, and three small panes of flat glass in

known world. Pliny makes a distinction between engraving executed by a hand tool and what he defines as the mechanical work achieved by the use of a wheel worked by a foot treadle and rotated in a lathe. (Nowadays a foot treadle would be regarded as decidedly old-fashioned.) The distinction is false. A wheel is no less a tool than a paintbrush or a chisel and whatever difference there is in quality between the one method and the other is due to the sensitivity and skill of the operator; a dull dog will execute a dull engraving, whatever method he uses. The simplest explanation of the process known to me is that provided by E. M. Elville in his *English Tableglass* (Country Life 1951). He is of course speaking of the world of today. 'The essential component is a

left Wine glass. Wheel-engraved with the monogram G.R., floral decoration and bunches of grapes. Drawn trumpet bowl. About 1730. Height $6\frac{1}{2}$ in. Garton Collection, London Museum.

right Goblet. Thistle bowl, wheel-engraved. Inverted-baluster stem with knops. About 1730. Height $7\frac{5}{8}$ in. Garton Collection, London Museum.

whether the honour for the revival should be given to Venice, Nuremberg or Antwerp that one may be excused a certain boredom. It is sufficient for most of us to remember that Italian workmen wandered far afield and that, if we care for such minutiae, the earliest German engraved vessel is a beaker at Prague dated 1566, the earliest Dutch one (also a beaker) is dated 1581, and the earliest English one (probably engraved by the Frenchman, Anthony de Lysle) is the Verzelini goblet of 1577.

Wheel engraving

43, 44, 45, 47 There is no special mystery associated with the technique of **wheel engraving** which, like diamond engraving, has been practised—with long intervals—since Rome was the centre of the

left Bowl. Diamond-point engraving. Arms of the Lane family, a hunting scene, birds and floral decoration. Early 18th century. Height 5¾ in. Garton Collection, London Museum.

right Silesian stem wine glass. Wheel-engraved in Holland. About 1715. Height 7 in.

product, not something from which other designs could be multiplied by the hundred.

Since the fall of the Roman Empire engraving on glass seems to have been in abeyance until the beginning of the 16th century, when it was revived by the Venetians. An early reference can be found in the work of the Bohemian priest Johannes Mathesius who wrote on glass manufacture in 1562, 'nowadays all sorts of festooning and handsome lines are drawn on the nice and bright Venetian glasses'. It is established that at the town of Hall in the Austrian Tyrol a glasshouse was founded in 1534, that a school of engravers was set up and, for a time, only Italian glassworkers were employed. There has been so much controversy about

Adam and Eve goblet engraved with diamond-point. About 1695. Ashmolean Museum, Oxford.

The Techniques of Engraving

Diamond engraving

Diamond engraving was used in England as early as the 16th century, and indeed it is the most obvious means by which glass can have a **design** scratched upon it. 'Scratched' is a homely word but that, in essence, is all that engraving implies whatever means are used. Diamond engraving in a linear style on table glass is seen on the Verzelini goblets in the British Museum, and on the **Amen glass** illustrated here. This is the method by which the artist, holding a tool containing a diamond or a steel point, scratches and taps upon the surface of the glass to make a design, the scratches making the highlights. Engraving in this manner goes back to the beginning of our era and is no more out of the way or mysterious than drawing a design on paper.

Stippling

The scratching can be, and often is, combined with a series of dots formed by striking the glass with a suitably mounted diamond — a refinement which demands much time and endless patience, and which was practised with conspicuous success by several Dutch artists, many of them amateurs, and now again, in our own century and with notable subtlety, by Laurence Whistler. The result is basically the same as the more familiar stipple engraving used for popular late 18th- and early 19th-century prints, though in that case the dots were made in a different manner on the copper plate from which the prints were pulled. Obviously a wine glass stipple-engraved is the end

39

glass of lead formula, with modifications and refinements, became standard for the better types of glass in England, the older, thinner, cheaper soda glass continued to be made. Moreover while glass of lead was greatly admired abroad, it did not—as did the inventions of Josiah Wedgwood in the pottery industry during the latter half of the 18th century—induce continental manufacturers to imitate it. It had many virtues, but glassmakers elsewhere already made fine glasses in their own manner and saw no reason to change. Where English glass of lead was superior was in its density, its ability to disperse the light passing through it, and—because of its density—its special suitability for engraving, which is why the Dutch engravers particularly favoured **glasses from Newcastle.**

left Newcastle wine glass. Wheel-engraved in Holland with the arms of William IV of Orange who married Anne, daughter of George II, in 1734. Height $7\frac{1}{2}$ in.

right Goblet. Newcastle glass, wheel-engraved in Holland. The inscription wishes happiness to the newly wedded Christina and Ysbrant Cardinaal. 18th April 1741. Height $8\frac{7}{8}$ in. Pilkington Museum of Glass, St Helens, Lancs.

Typical early 18th-century glasses.

They were probably made in Dublin in about 1720. One is engraved with a portrait of William III in a medallion below a border of Baroque scrollwork. Above is the legend 'THE GLORIOUS AND IMMORTALL MEMORY OF KING WILL III' and below 'HE WAS BUT WORDS ARE WANTING TO SAY WHAT SAY ALL THATS GREAT AND GOOD AND HE WAS THAT'. The other beneath a similar border has a portrait, also in a medallion, flanked by the letters 'W R' and the inscription 'THE GLORIOUS AND IMMORTAL MEMORY OF KING WILLIAM AND HIS QUEEN MARY'. As with the similar glasses praising King James they too have attracted the attention of the faker. It so happens that during the year 1962–1963 both a Williamite and an Old Pretender goblet were sold at Sotheby's. The former was of mammoth size, $12\frac{1}{2}$ inches in height, and engraved with an equestrian portrait of the king and inscribed 'THE GLORIOUS AND IMMORTAL MEMORY OF KING WILLIAM AND HIS QUEEN MARY AND PERPETUAL DISAPPOINTMENT TO THE POPE THE PRETENDER AND ALL THE ENEMIES OF THE PROTESTANT RELIGION'. The Old Pretender goblet, $9\frac{1}{2}$ inches high, was engraved with the customary cypher J.R. and the words:

'Send Him soon home
To Holyruood House and that no Sooner
than I do with Vive La Roy'

—admirable sentiments if faulty English and French. However, the commemoration could occasionally turn out to be quite humorous (if unintentionally so) as the comic **portrait of William III** on one 18th-century wine glass shows.

The years then from about 1690 to the 1740s were mainly concerned with comparatively humdrum, though vastly important tasks. Dozens of anonymous glassmakers scattered up and down the country consolidated the technical achievements of Ravenscroft. As yet we know very little of either the individuals or of the various glasshouses which gradually built up the industry, and it is not unreasonable to assume that many local records await patient scrutiny. The Ravenscroft breakthrough must none the less be seen in perspective. While the

reverse. It is tempting to see in this a direct allusion to the Old Pretender, a dark-visaged man, but the more sceptical among us prefer to reserve judgment. It is at least possible that such a glass could have been a purely private and personal celebration for, say, the christening of a boy called James, with a blackbird added as a pretty decoration with no hidden meaning whatever.

Williamite glasses are the inevitable reply to Jacobite glasses, though, unlike the latter, they can hardly be said to constitute so sentimental and nostalgic a cult. Two typical examples, neither of them remarkable for their engraving, are illustrated by Thorpe in *A History of English and Irish Glass* (London 1927), each with a drawn stem enclosing a tear, trumpet bowl and folded foot.

Goblet, commemorating the Battle of the Boyne, 1690. King William III with cavalry and infantry crossing the river. Early 18th century. Height $9\frac{1}{4}$ in.

take a dim view of the house of Hanover. A long time ago I found myself in conversation with a woman at Windsor; as we were about to enter the State Apartments she touched my arm and whispered conspiratorially, 'Do you think it is right for me to go round? You see, I'm a convinced Jacobite.' I assured her she was in no danger from the brutal English government!

The engraving, it should be added, on Amen glasses is diamond-point, not wheel engraving. One glass (a soda glass, not glass of lead), recorded by E. Barrington Haynes in his book *Glass Through the Ages* (London 1948), could perhaps be as early as 1715 and is hardly later than 1735. This bears the inscription 'A Halth to I...ms', and what appears to be a blackbird on the

Flask decorated with 'nipped diamond waies'. The silver collar is inscribed 'Thomas Burrowes 1700'. Victoria and Albert Museum, London.

It is scarcely necessary to issue a warning against forgeries, the most dangerous among them those on which engraving by an outrageously accomplished modern hand has been added to genuine drawn-stem glasses of about the mid 18th century.

All these glasses commemorate old, unhappy, far-off things, but it is surprising what a number of people are still to be found who cling nostalgically to the mystique of the 'divine right of kings', and to the romantic picture of Charles Edward as the would-be saviour of the country. Only recently (1969) a reception was held in London to commemorate the centenary of the birth of Prince Ruprecht of Bavaria, the last representative of the royal house of Stuart. Occasionally one meets dedicated persons who

Salver on ribbed stem and domed foot, with glasses for sweets. The 1720s. Victoria and Albert Museum, London.

Jacobite goblet. Wheel-engraved with the portrait of the Old Pretender, James III. About 1715-1720. Height 8 in. Corning Museum of Glass, Corning, New York.

the ingenious theory that these at least could be dated to the years 1720 to 1727 and had been made to commemorate the birth of either Charles Edward (Bonnie Prince Charlie) or his brother Henry, who became a cardinal. But most scholars now agree that this is a misinterpretation of the word *increase*, which refers not to the number of members of the house of Stuart but to the family's influence and power. There are at least three dated Amen glasses, each of them an expression of purely personal loyalty to the cause, but not one of these is from before Culloden. These are the Dunvegan castle glass of 1747 and the glasses of 1749 from Mesham and Drummond castles.

Jacobite bowl. Rose and single bud and butterfly. Wheel-engraved. First half of the 18th century. Diameter $3\frac{1}{2}$ in. Garton Collection, London Museum.

wheel-engraved specimens. Whether pre- or post-Culloden the Jacobite anthem—sometimes in two verses only—is as follows:

God Save the King, I pray,
God Bliss the King, I pray,
　God Save the King.
Send Him Victorious,
Happy and Glorious,
Soon to reign over us,
　God Save the King.

God Bliss the subjects all,
And save both great and small
　In every station,
That will bring home the King
Who has best right to reign,
It is the only thing
　Can save the Nation.

God Bliss the Prince of Wales,
The true born Prince of Wales,
　Sent us by Thee.
Grant us one favour more
The King for to restore
As Thou has done before
　The familie.

God Save the Church, I pray,
And Bliss the Church, I pray,
　Pure to remain,
Against all Heresie
And Whigs' Hypocrisie,
Who strive maliciously
　Her to defame.

A few of the Amen glasses have engraved upon them the words 'To the Increase of the Royal Familie', which has led to

Edward after the disaster of Culloden. The view taken here, largely on grounds of style, is that at least a few of the two dozen Amen glasses recorded may have been made after the 1715 attempt at restoration and before 1745. It is likely that the problem will never be solved to the satisfaction of everyone, but what is certain is that **drawn-stem trumpet glasses**, whether of Jacobite interest or no, whether with a tear or an airtwist, are among the best things English glassmakers produced. As for Jacobite glasses in general they continue to interest collectors because, even after more than two centuries, they have an emotional appeal which has nothing to do with their aesthetic merit. That, it must be confessed, is frequently abysmal. Though nearly all of them were produced after the final defeat at Culloden in 1746, certain Amen glasses are perhaps earlier, as are a few

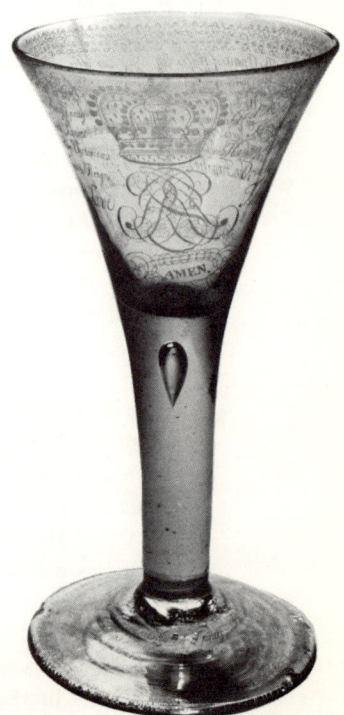

Amen glass. Drawn stem and trumpet bowl. Diamond-engraved with the royal crown and cypher and the words of the Jacobite national anthem. Ashmolean Museum, Oxford.

Drawn Stems and Amen Glasses

If the dignified heavy baluster-stem glasses of these years hold pride of place, followed at a little distance by the Silesian stems, there is a third type which many consider should be bracketed equal. This is the graceful drawn stem, where the stem is not made separately but is drawn out from a trumpet-shaped bowl in one piece. It is a simple, harmonious shape, known to Venice years previously. It was first known in western and northern Europe in the 17th century when the basic form was slender, becoming more massive in the time of Queen Anne and George I, and then lighter again in the middle of the 18th century.

Both baluster stems and these drawn stems frequently enclose an air bubble or tear, and in several the air bubble or bubbles are developed into an air-twist—a very pretty trick indeed, which seems to have been an English invention. Such glasses were advertised as early as 1737 as 'wormed glasses' or 'wrought glasses'. Of all the drawn-stem glasses the most famous are a few, a very few, diamond-engraved with the cypher of James, the Old Pretender (J.R. 8), and two or more verses of the Jacobite anthem, ending with the word 'Amen'. These are always referred to as Amen glasses and they all appear to belong to the years 1720 to 1745. There has however been a certain amount of controversy about them in recent years, one theory going so far as to suggest that all of them, whether they refer to the Old Pretender or to his son, are later than the final collapse of Jacobite hopes during the 1745 campaign and the escape of Prince Charles

the materials from which they were made. (The late W.B. Honey in his invaluable *Glass* which deals with the collection at the Victoria and Albert Museum and is a repository of wisdom besides, notes that broken glass, especially of the 17th century and later, is seen only rarely in London excavations whereas fragments of pottery and porcelain are found in quantity). But if actual specimens are extremely rare, documentary evidence is not lacking. For instance, a sale of German cut glass was advertised in London in 1709, but 'was interrupted by the great disturbance made by some Glass Sellers of London whereby the auction could not be carried on'. Another advertisement of 1737, by Jerom Johnson, announces 'all manner of cut glass' including 'Scallop'd Desart Glasses in the newest fashion'.

left Goblet. Hollow six-sided, star-studded Silesian stem. Height $7\frac{3}{4}$ in.

right Candlestick. Eight-sided, semi-solid Silesian stem. Large studs on the shoulder above; below this knops containing rows of tears. Larger studs on the domed foot. About 1720. Height $9\frac{3}{4}$ in. Pilkington Museum of Glass, St Helens, Lancs.

The other influence which was continental (German-Austrian-Bohemian) in origin was that of wheel engraving and cutting, but very little of this survives from these years. The extreme rarity of glasses of this sort has long puzzled historians. The explanation generally adopted is that while such glasses must have been made they were not fashionable until the middle of the century, and therefore would have been among the first to have been broken up and re-used as 'cullet' for the furnaces. Glass fragments could often be bought for less than the cost of

far left Mead glass. Cup-shaped bowl, plain stem beneath a double collar. About 1695. Height $6\frac{1}{4}$ in

left Silesian stem goblet. About 1720. Height $9\frac{1}{2}$ in.

right Wine glass. Silesian stem. Inscribed on the shoulder 'God Save King George'. About 1715-1730. Height $6\frac{1}{4}$ in. Garton Collection, London Museum.

24, 25, 26, 27
candlesticks with one or other of the several variations of the inverted-baluster stem, of the first thirty or forty years of the century. There was however a form of stem which could vie with the more usual baluster in comeliness—the so-called **Silesian stem**, high-shouldered and ribbed, which came into fashion partly as a result of the Treaty of Utrecht in 1713 which opened up the markets of western Europe to German products after the long wars, and more especially because of the accession of George I from Hanover in the following year.

It is necessary to emphasise that, on the whole, during the fifty years covered by this book, the English glassmakers evolved a style which was wholly their own and which can be compared with that of the silversmiths during the reigns of Queen Anne and George I—a style in which smooth surfaces and fine well-balanced proportions are left to speak for themselves without the aid of other decoration. This is not to suggest that there was no influence from abroad, but that the main emphasis was on a use of metal which can be described as lavish in terms of weight and for which its lustrous, almost oily quality was peculiarly suited. Most of us confess to a prejudice in favour of the generous simple forms of the goblets, wine glasses and

22, 23   Two more glasses, a **goblet** and a **tazza**, are also from very early in the century and have two features in common: moulded gadroon decoration and a bobbin stem. The eight-knopped stem of the goblet contains an elongated tear (not a cut as one might imagine from the photograph), while the stem of the tazza is composed of four graduated knops. Like so many others illustrated here, the **mead glass** dating from 1695 was once in the well known collection of the late Walter Smith of Trenton, New Jersey. Again, gadroon decoration can be found on the lower part of the cup-shaped bowl which rests on a double collar and a plain column. The whole has a curiously gawky, leggy look which is somehow not quite mature.

24

left Goblet. Gadroon moulded bowl, bobbin stem of eight knops containing an elongated tear. About 1700. Height $5\frac{3}{4}$ in.

right Tazza. Gadroon moulded, the stem composed of four graduated knops. About 1710. Height $3\frac{1}{2}$ in.

Candlestick. Hollow baluster stem with tear above two knops, domed and terraced foot. Early 18th century. Height 6¾ in.

Sweetmeat glass. Bowl with gadrooned base and everted rim. Double-knopped stem, folded conical foot. Early 18th century. Height 3⅝ in.

Cordial glass. Cylinder stem with a tear. About 1700. Height 6 in.

Wine glass with the inscription 'PROSPERITY TO IRELAND', and floral and bird border. Columnar stem. About 1720. Height 6½ in.

Wine glass. Flared trumpet bowl on unusual double-collared, knopped stem, domed foot. About 1710. Height 6¼ in.

Wine glass. Drawn stem, slender baluster. About 1725. Height 7 in. Victoria and Albert Museum, London.

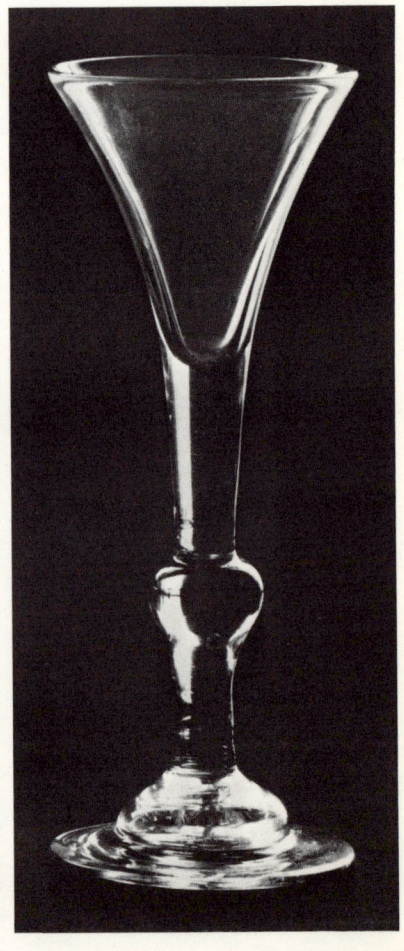

Acorn baluster wine glass. Teared baluster over a teared acorn-knopped stem, conical foot. About 1710. Height 8¼ in.

Tavern glass. Inverted-baluster stem containing a large tear, folded conical foot. About 1695. Height 7 in.

Wine glass. Funnel bowl. Hollow stem, an acorn above a spherical knop. About 1700. Height 7 in.

Ale glass. Tall funnel bowl. Double-knopped stem, wide folded foot. About 1695. Height 6½ in.

With the next goblet we are on solid ground once again; solid in every way, for here is the typical **heavy inverted-baluster type** of the early years of the 18th century, with the addition of the words, engraved in diamond-point, 'God Bless Queen Ann' who, it will be remembered, came to the throne in 1702 and died in 1714. This wonderfully satisfying glass provides a substantial, comfortable base from which to consider the changes rung upon this simple shape during the years 1700 to 1740, from, say, the wine glass with the **bell bowl** of about 1700 with its decidedly clumsy, gawky proportions, the **baluster goblet** with the beautiful thistle bowl, hollow mushroom and ball-knopped stem, made some five years later, to the **goblet of about 1740**, wheel-engraved round the rim and bearing the Walpole family motto, and the stem facet-cut. In between is a representative array which can be seen in the **illustrations**.

Wine glass. Bell bowl solid at the base; drop knop baluster stem, cushion knop above folded conical foot. About 1700. Height $6\frac{3}{8}$ in.

were intended. The no less elegant **goblet and cover** in the London Museum is also ascribed to the years 1715–1730, again on grounds of style. Few things are more difficult to photograph than very small details in glass where reflections can play very odd tricks indeed. In this case the cover finial is a man in a tricorne hat, presumably a portrait of John Churchill, first Duke of Marlborough, who died in 1722. This, for obvious reasons, leads one to that oddity in the Guildhall Museum, the **drinking-device for birds**, crowned by a man's head also wearing a tricorne hat (the so-called Ramillies hat). It is an amusing survival, and there appears to be some evidence that it was one of several made by a certain T. Meyer in about 1705.

prove that the glass cannot have been made before their date, *not*—emphatically not—that the glass was made in the same year. The second **wine glass** is thought to come from between the years 1715 and 1730, mainly because of its style (the easy, flared curve of the bowl is a particularly attractive feature) but possibly because it contains a James II threepenny piece of 1687. In other words it is just possible that after the disappointment of Stuart hopes in 1715, some supporter of the Old Pretender (to the faithful, King James III) had a coin from his father's reign inserted into the glass while it was being blown. But as I note later in speaking of Jacobite glasses, it is not difficult, once one is sufficiently devout, to see references to the lost cause where none

Painted goblet. The initials 'L.H.' enclosed in a red circle surmounted by an owl; floral decoration and various birds. About 1710. Height $9\frac{1}{4}$ in. Garton Collection, London Museum.

right Wine glass. The knop contains a James II threepenny piece of 1687. About 1715–1730. Height $8\frac{7}{8}$ in. Garton Collection, London Museum.

far right Drinking device for birds. Blown and moulded, with man's head wearing a tricorne hat. Perhaps by T. Meyer, about 1705. Height 6 in. Guildhall Museum, London.

Goblet. Pincered ornament. Blown knop with applied prunts. Threepenny piece of 1679 in the knop. Early 18th century. Height $9\frac{1}{2}$ in. Garton Collection, London Museum.

Wine glass. About 1695. Height $6\frac{3}{4}$ in.

layer of glass), or domed and folded, at first rather thin as was the usual practice in Venice, but later wide and thick in harmony with the proportions of the vessel as a whole.

In a book of this type it is obviously impossible to indicate more than a few standard, and some very rare variations of stem, bowl and foot. A hasty glance detects little essential difference between them, but a closer look will show an apparently infinite capacity on the part of their makers to think up some slight alteration to the norm. It is just this imaginative quality in nearly all these vessels, which were mostly made for daily use and not merely for ornament, that makes their study so fascinating. For example, **two noble goblets** from the Victoria and Albert Museum, the one covered, the other uncovered, both from the last few years of the 17th century and one imagines from the same factory, differ in the most subtle manner. The latter has a flared lip, a knop above a collar, and a wider, flatter foot than its neighbour, with its domed and folded foot and inverted-baluster stem. Each is a far more elegant product than the dumpy, but eminently practical, not easily broken **glass with a domed foot**, also from the same period.

Other pretty tricks from early 18th-century practice are worth attention. An **extraordinary rarity** for an English glass of the early 18th century is one painted with the letters L.H. enclosed in a red circle, surmounted by an owl and with various birds and floral decoration. Three more examples from this period all have prunts applied round the central knop—an engaging fashion familiar enough in the German and Netherlandish glasses known as *roemers*, so frequently seen in Dutch and Flemish still-life paintings. They were originally applied to the short wide stems of these vessels for purely practical reasons, to prevent the fingers from slipping on the smooth surface, but here their presence is no more than decorative, hardly more than a foil to the gleaming perfection of the metal itself and to the elegant proportions of the vessels they enrich. Although the knop of the first example contains a threepenny piece dated 1679, the **style and metal** of this glass belong to the early 18th century. Coins are not infrequently found embedded in glasses; they

Goblet and cover. Late 17th century. Height 14 in. Victoria and Albert Museum, London.

likely to quarrel with the descriptions first suggested by A. Hartshorne as long ago as 1897 in his pioneering study *Old English Glasses*—descriptions which are still accepted as valid. He divides the bowls into eleven categories: flanged, round-funnel, ovoid, ogee, double ogee, flute, conical, cup, trumpet, bucket and bell. In general, in the early, pre-1700 years the straight-sided bowl was in favour, with the waisted bowl, as stems became more elaborate, beginning to take its place.

While both stem and bowl obviously lent themselves to numerous modifications, the foot presented a more difficult problem and from the time of Ravenscroft until about 1730 at least was either folded (the rim folded under the base to form a double

left Ale glass. Tall bowl on collar above small spherical knop, true baluster stem, folded conical foot. About 1710. Height $8\frac{1}{4}$ in.

right Wine glass. Almost thistle bowl, mushroom knop, then straight section above base knop. Folded conical foot. About 1705. Height $6\frac{3}{8}$ in.

Variations on Several Themes

As the years passed fashion decreed that stems should be longer, so the normal, rather stubby baluster stem was lengthened by the addition of knops in bewildering variety. Indeed, the permutations and combinations existed in such variety that while many in the past have endeavoured to analyse the different types and to place them in some kind of logical order no one, as far as I am aware, has succeeded. As a rough guide one may accept, as the most probable approximation to the truth, the opinion expressed by the late E.M. Elville in his *English Tableglass* (Country Life 1951). He suggests the following dates for the birth and death of the nine chief variations on the baluster theme. Naturally he made no claim to be speaking *ex cathedra* but most collectors seem to agree that the list is as good a guide to probabilities as exists.

57	**Inverted baluster**	1682–1710
	Drop knop	1690–1710
	Angular knop	1695–1715
	Ball knop	1695–1715
	Annulated or triple-ring knop	1700–1725
	Multiple knops	1700–1720
10	**True baluster**	1710–1730
	Acorn knop	1710–1715
10	**Mushroom knop**	1710–1715

While the stem was the most obvious place in which to pursue variety the bowl also lent itself to experiment. Again no one is

dependent upon the splendour of the metal itself with its power of reflecting light. To many, and in spite of later developments (air-twist stems, wheel engraving, cutting, opaque twists, colour twists and many others), the goblets and wine glasses from the early years of the 18th century are beyond compare—substantial, well-balanced, well-bred shapes, at first with **short**, soon with **longer stems**, all adapted from the classical architectural ornament the baluster, in most cases, in England, the inverted baluster.

left Goblet. About 1690–1700. Height 12 in. British Museum, London.

right Goblet. A common tear through the several knops. About 1700. Height $11\frac{1}{4}$ in. Pilkington Museum of Glass, St Helens, Lancs.

all 18th-century and later glass he will be less handicapped. It is not that prices are likely to fall, but at least 18th-century glass, and more especially 18th-century wine glasses, have survived in considerable numbers and in **great variety** and by no means all are in public collections—at least not yet.

An indication of the industry's expansion during the last quarter of the 17th century is provided by John Houghton, who published in 1696 a series of articles on the subject of glass and thoughtfully added a careful list of the various glasshouses grouped according to the type of product manufactured. He mentions twenty-five towns or districts in which glass manufacture of one kind or another was carried on. London was the main centre with twenty-four, Stourbridge the second with seventeen, Newcastle-on-Tyne the third with eleven, and the Bristol district the fourth with nine. Naturally the majority made ordinary **glass bottles**, window glass and so forth. Thus in his London list, Houghton classifies nine glasshouses as making bottle glass, two as making looking-glass plates, four crown glass and plate (window glass), and nine 'flint and ordinary', by which he presumably means glass of lead in two styles, light and heavy. The heavy, as time went on, proved the more popular, no doubt because it was less easily broken and could stand up to ordinary household hazards better than its more delicate, cheaper companions, and, of course, was far more robust than the soda glass of Venice and elsewhere.

The result of these late 17th-century experiments, then, was to establish a widespread industry unhampered by monopolist financiers (as it had been under the Stuarts), and a basic material of good quality which lent itself admirably to the comparatively sober fashions of the time but was too weighty and, in its molten state, too viscous, to allow craftsmen to play the pretty tricks in manipulating it that had so impressed the world in the work of the Venetian glasshouses. One can almost assert that the metal (the common term for glass in its worked and unworked state) so nearly perfected by Ravenscroft, and improved since his death, imposed its own discipline upon its followers, inevitably compelling them to concentrate on **massive, dignified forms**,

view of the collector. So little has survived from the 16th and 17th centuries that it is unlikely that the average private individual will see more than a dozen or so authentic pieces from these years actually on the market, and if he does, it is still more unlikely that he will be able to compete with the well-heeled persons and institutions who will inevitably be in pursuit. With

left Goblet and cover. The cover is surmounted by a portrait thought to be of John Churchill, first Duke of Marlborough. The knop in the cover contains a Queen Anne fourpenny piece of 1708; the one in the stem a Queen Anne shilling of 1714. About 1715-1730. Height $12\frac{7}{8}$ in. with the cover. Garton Collection, London Museum.

right Wine glass. Inverted baluster stem with air bubble. About 1700. Height 5 in. Garton Collection, London Museum.

by myriads of little lines, but this fault was corrected after some years by a proper balance of lead in the mixture, and so the characteristic English 'glass of lead' came into normal production. For the first time England became self-supporting and an exporter of glass. By a coincidence Germany and Bohemia freed themselves from the dominance of Venice at about the same time, by purifying their hitherto Venetian-inspired glass by the addition of lime in suitable proportions.

In future the story of the glass industry in England is more fragmented, less amenable to the broad treatment inevitably given to its past, and less dominated by a few exceptional personalities. But there is this great advantage from the point of

Goblet. Late 17th century. Height 9 in. Victoria and Albert Museum, London.

that he may soon be finding more satisfactory supplies at home, from which one can deduce that important developments were to be expected. They came perhaps sooner than Greene or his fellow members of the Glass-sellers' Company dared to hope. The Company was evidently composed of a nucleus of forward-looking members who could see the advantages which might accrue to them if they no longer had to rely upon imports and so backed the experiments which George Ravenscroft began in 1673 at his glasshouse in the Savoy. He employed Italian craftsmen as his assistants and made sufficient progress to encourage his backers to finance further experiments at Henley-on-Thames. His early glasses were liable to 'crizzle', that is to become clouded

Wine glass. Moulded trumpet bowl, domed and folded foot. About 1730. Height 7 in. Pilkington Museum of Glass, St Helens, Lancs.

The New Metal

Numbers in the margin refer to the page where an illustration may be found

This book deals with English table glass from the end of the 17th century to about 1745. These dates are convenient, the latter because of the imposition of taxation on glassmakers, and the first because it was at that time that the discoveries of George Ravenscroft began to be put into practice over a wide area, and a distinctive English metal for the better type of glass became normal. Until then Venice had been supreme in the world of glass and when good quality glass was made in England it was Venetian both in material and manner – that is, soda glass. Indeed, experts are extremely cautious in attributing any apparently early or mid 17th-century glasses to an English glasshouse. All that is certain is that Venetian glasses were imported in quantity during these years, that the Netherlands made similar not to say identical wine glasses and goblets, and when such things are seen either in a collection or more rarely at an auction they are generally described as façon de Venise.

Some definite facts are provided later in the 17th century (1667–1672) by the records of a firm of London glass-sellers, John Greene and Michael Measey, which are preserved in the British Museum. During these years they imported over one thousand looking-glass plates (mirror glass) and two thousand dozen glasses, and the correspondence from Greene to his supplier, Alessio Morelli of Murano, the island which was, and still is, the centre of the Venetian glass industry, is largely concerned with complaints about quality and breakages. In 1671 he warns